Elizabeth Ann Seton

Mother for Many

1774–1821
Born in New York, New York
First American-born saint
Feast Day: January 4
Patronage: Catholic schools

Text by Barbara Yoffie
Illustrated by Katherine A. Borgatti

Liguori

Dedication

**To my family:
my parents Jim and Peg,
my husband Bill,
our son Sam and daughter-in-law Erin,
and our precious grandchildren
Ben, Lucas, and Andrew**

**To all the children I have had the privilege of
teaching throughout the years.**

Imprimi Potest:
Harry Grile, CSsR, Provincial
Denver Province, The Redemptorists

Published by Liguori Publications
Liguori, Missouri 63057

To order, call 800-325-9521
www.liguori.org

p ISBN 978-0-7648-2241-4
e ISBN 978-0-7648-6832-0

Liguori Publications, a nonprofit corporation, is an apostolate of The
Redemptorists. To learn more about The Redemptorists, visit Redemptorists.com.

Printed in the United States of America
17 16 15 14 13 / 5 4 3 2 1
First Edition

Dear Parents and Teachers:

Saints and Me! is a series of children's books about saints. Six books make up the first set: *Saints of North America.* In this set, each book tells a thought-provoking story about a heavenly hero.

Saints of North America includes the heroic lives of six saints from the United States, Canada, and Mexico. Saints Kateri Tekakwitha and Elizabeth Ann Seton were both born in the United States. Saint Juan Diego was born in Mexico, and Saint André Bessette was from Canada. European missionaries also came to North America to spread the Catholic faith, making it their home while they worked with people in the New World. Saints Rose Philippine Duchesne and Damien de Veuster were missionary saints.

Through the centuries, saints have always been dear to Catholics, but *why?* In most instances, ordinary people were and are transformed by the life of Jesus and therefore model Christ's life for us. It is our Lord who makes ordinary people extraordinary. As your children come to know the saints, it is our hope that they will come to understand and identify that they, too, are *called to be saints*.

Which saint wanted to work with Native Americans? Who wanted to work with the sick people on the island of Molokai, Hawaii? To which saint did the Virgin Mary appear? Who loved Saint Joseph? Which saint started the first American religious community of women? Do you know which saint is the patron of nature? Find the answers in the *Saints of North America, Saints and Me!* set and help your child identify with the lives of the saints.

Introduce your children or students to the *Saints and Me!* series as they:

—READ about the lives of the saints and are inspired by their stories.

—PRAY to the saints for their intercession.

—CELEBRATE the saints and relate to their lives.

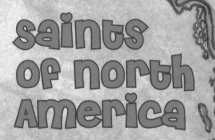

saints of north America

 Kateri Tekakwitha

 Juan Diego

 Rose Philippine Duchesne

 Damien of Molokai

 Elizabeth Ann Seton

 André Bessette

Belgium

France

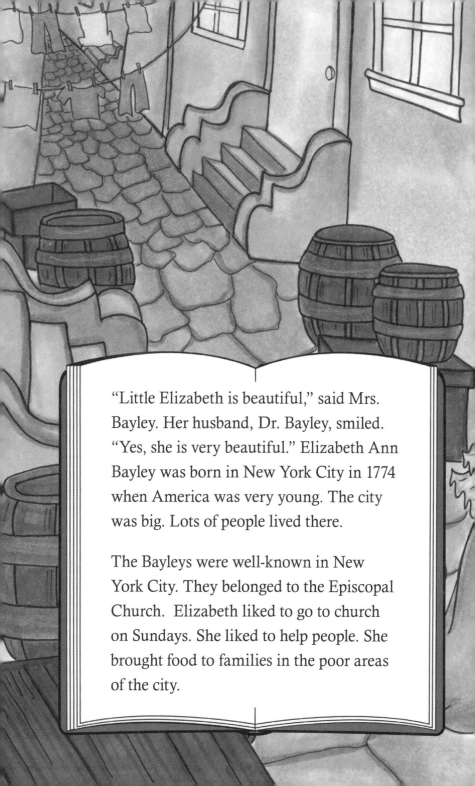

"Little Elizabeth is beautiful," said Mrs. Bayley. Her husband, Dr. Bayley, smiled. "Yes, she is very beautiful." Elizabeth Ann Bayley was born in New York City in 1774 when America was very young. The city was big. Lots of people lived there.

The Bayleys were well-known in New York City. They belonged to the Episcopal Church. Elizabeth liked to go to church on Sundays. She liked to help people. She brought food to families in the poor areas of the city.

School was fun. She liked to draw and play the piano. Elizabeth learned how to speak French. "I love to read books!" said Elizabeth. "I want to read all the books in my father's library!"

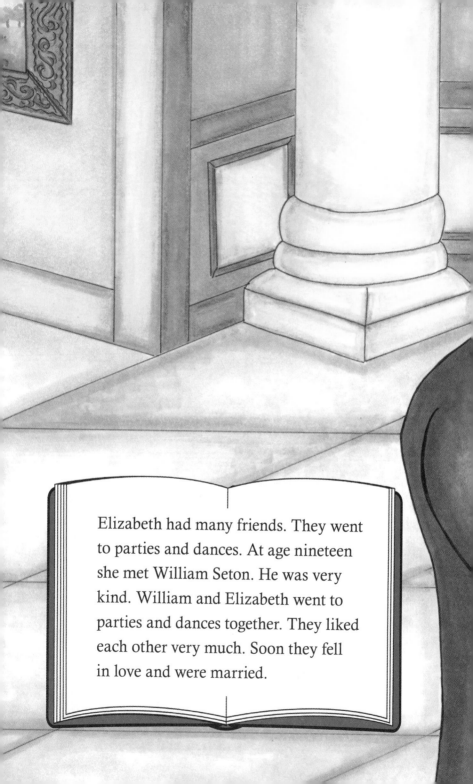

Elizabeth had many friends. They went to parties and dances. At age nineteen she met William Seton. He was very kind. William and Elizabeth went to parties and dances together. They liked each other very much. Soon they fell in love and were married.

Life was happy for the Seton family. They had five children. William worked in the family shipping business. Elizabeth took care of the children and did charity work. Then one day their happy life changed.

William's business closed. The family could not pay their bills. Then William got sick. He had tuberculosis. "God will help us," Elizabeth told her family. "The Lord will help us through our troubles."

Elizabeth and William went to
Italy. "The warm weather might
help William's sickness," thought
Elizabeth. She prayed that he would
get better. But William did not get
better. He died and Elizabeth was
now a widow.

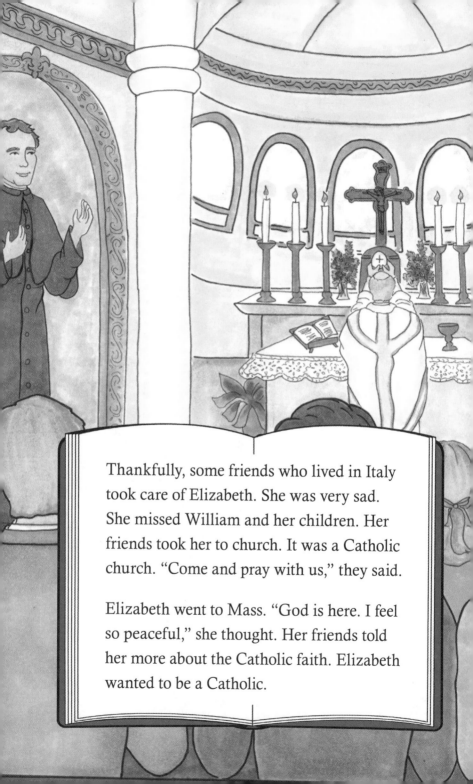

Thankfully, some friends who lived in Italy took care of Elizabeth. She was very sad. She missed William and her children. Her friends took her to church. It was a Catholic church. "Come and pray with us," they said.

Elizabeth went to Mass. "God is here. I feel so peaceful," she thought. Her friends told her more about the Catholic faith. Elizabeth wanted to be a Catholic.

She returned to New York. There were so many things to do! Being a single parent was hard. It was also hard to leave the Episcopal Church. Elizabeth and her children converted to the Catholic faith. Her friends and family stopped talking to her.

A priest asked Elizabeth to start
a Catholic school in Baltimore,
Maryland. Now she could help her
children and other children, too.
She could see God's plan for her.

Elizabeth was a good teacher and leader.
She started a religious community.
They were called the Sisters of Charity
of Saint Joseph. It was the first
American religious community.
"We will teach the children about God,"
she told the sisters.

The sisters moved to Emmitsburg,
Maryland. Elizabeth's children moved
with her so she could take care of them.
Her religious community needed her,
too. She became the mother superior.
Everyone called her Mother Seton.

Mother Seton and the other sisters
worked very hard. They started a school
for poor children. It was the first Catholic
school in the United States. The sisters
opened more schools and orphanages
in Philadelphia and New York City.

More women joined the Sisters of Charity. The religious community spread to other big cities in the United States. The sisters helped the sick in hospitals. They cared for children in orphanages. They taught children in schools.

Mother Seton died of tuberculosis on January 4, 1821. Today the Sisters of Charity teach and help people around the world.

Saint Elizabeth Ann Seton prayed for strength during sad times in her life. We can ask God for help when we are worried or sad.

In happy times and sad times, too, God is always close to you.

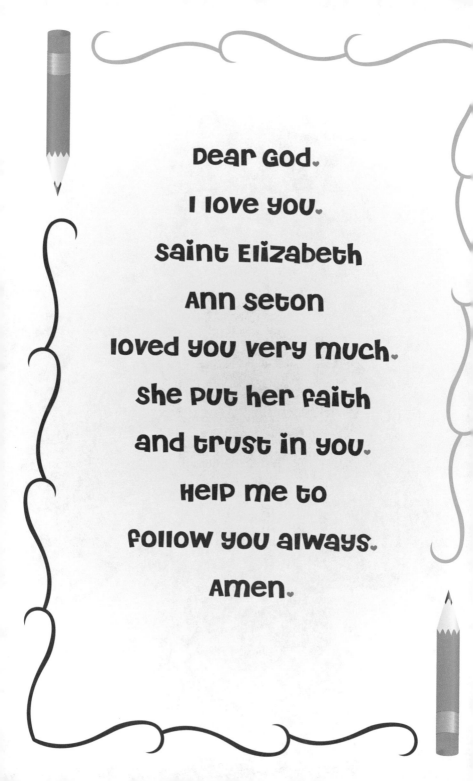

Dear God,

I love you.

Saint Elizabeth

Ann Seton

loved you very much.

She put her faith

and trust in you.

Help me to

follow you always.

Amen.

NEW WORDS (Glossary)

Convert: A person who goes through a change of heart about his or her religious beliefs

Episcopal Church: A Protestant church. Protestant churches have some different beliefs than the Catholic Church.

Mother: The superior or leader of a group of women religious

Orphanage: A home for children who do not have parents

Religious community: A group of men or women who witness to the faith and take vows (promises). They are called priests, brothers, monks, friars, sisters, or nuns.

Sisters of Charity: A group of women religious founded in the United States by Elizabeth Ann Seton in 1809

Tuberculosis: A serious lung illness

Widow: A woman whose husband has died

Liguori Publications
saints and me! series
SAINTS OF NORTH AMERICA

Kateri Tekakwitha
Model of Bravery

Juan Diego
Mary's Humble Messenger

Rose Philippine Duchesne
A Dreamer and a Missionary

Damien of Molokai
Builder of Community

André Bessette
A Heart of Strength

SAINTS OF NORTH AMERICA ACTIVITY BOOK
Reproducible activities for all 6 saints in the series